I've Got a Crush

Poems & Essays

Sue Schafer

I've Got a Crush

Copyright © 2012 by Sue Schafer

ISBN 9780615595979

Table of Contents

I've Got a Crush

I got a crush in a bad way
I don't even know him
I find myself looking for him
Hoping for a chance encounter
It's crazy
I feel possessed
Obsessed
Helpless
Most of all I feel
  gratitude
Gratitude for the energy
The constant buzz
The glow in my cheeks
The sparkle in my eyes
It sounds too corny
All I know is that
  it's happening to me
I go through the day
  in a bubble of anticipation
Everything is new
Vibrant
Interesting *

He's Intoxicating

He's intoxicating
Beguiling
Bewitching
I touch him
Smell him
Hold him all day
He haunts my dreams
Dominates my thoughts
I take him everywhere
Talk to him all day
It feels so good
  to have a constant companion
Who worships me
Who doesn't question me
Who always finds me
  immensely amusing and sensitive
I know it's not right
I know it won't go anywhere
But I can't stop myself
I don't want to
I know he wouldn't want to
if he felt this way too *

Why Can't I Forget

Why can't I forget
looking into your eyes
and feeling touched
in places I never knew existed?
Why can't I stop longing
to look into your eyes again?
Why can't my body stop
basking in the heat
of your presence
as if you were near?
I feel like a child
Confused
by
my
excitement *

I Know I Saw You

I know I
saw you today
I think you saw me

I know you
are thinking about me
because
I'm thinking about you

I know we
need to talk
because
I've been talking
to you *

My Body Feels Raw

My body feels raw
open
on fire
I want to tear off my clothes
sprawl on my back
close my eyes
drift far
far away
this yearning is unbearable
my eyes constantly search for yours
my skin awaits your touch
my nose longs for your scent
it's as if
my whole being needs you now
wants you beyond reason
somehow
in some way *

Sue Schafer

I Am Certain

I am certain
that if I had
just one more day
on the planet
the Universe would give me
the words to describe
the gratitude I feel everyday
when I think of you
You mean more to me
than you will ever know
You reside in my heart
in my soul
You have changed my life
in ways you will never know
I speak your name everyday
and ask the Universe
to bless you
and give you peace *

I Can't Tell You

I can't tell you
will never tell you
how important you are
to my life
I bring you to my mind
whenever I want to feel
my body tremble
I feel your mouth press
against mine
your arms hold me tightly
I feel weak
I want you too badly
too urgently
I can't help but part my legs
press my hips
it's shameful
it's wild
it's uncontrollable *

Sue Schafer

I Crossed Over

I crossed over
into
your
soul

I know
you
felt
me

I know
you
feel
me
now *

I Feel the Preciousness

I feel the preciousness
of this moment
so keenly that
I know
I'll think back
and wonder
if I knew
that
this
was
to be
our
last
moment
together *

Sue Schafer

I Love Your Smile

I love your smile and the way your eyes sparkle
You stood off the trail and held your dog
I wanted to stop and chat but didn't
You are the portal to another life
A life we'll never share
I weave your energy with mine
Like you weave mine
It feels right
Very sexy
Very real
Like it was
meant
to
be *

I Don't Know Why

I don't know why I didn't stop to chit chat
I felt awkward
transparent
guilty
most of all, guilty
guilty for thinking about you
guilty for making love to you
guilty for touching you
guilty for using you so lewdly
I didn't want you to sense my secret

If I were single I most certainly would have stopped
I would have walked with you
followed you home
had a glass of water
a bite to eat
this attraction is too powerful
too uncontrollable
too unexplainable
too dangerous
to risk exposure *

The Need

The need
is immediate
undeniable
uncontrollable

the need to
touch
dominate
tame

it's no less
than
primal

images
of me

images
of you

desire
fear
longing
lust *

We Are Connected

We are connected
you and I
we both
feel it
know it
avoid it *

Sue Schafer

Men In My Orbit

Men in my orbit is not unusual
It's always amusing and arousing and fun
A little harmless game

Until today

At first I wasn't sure what was happening
I was spellbound, riveted in place
Electricity jolted my body
and then I noticed something strange
You hadn't notice me
How could you have not seen me
Sensed me like I sensed you
Isn't that the way it works
Isn't that the way it has always worked
I was crushed
Now I can't get you out of my mind
I find myself seeking you out
Going back to where I had seen you
Going to new places
Driving in new directions
I get dressed with you in mind
I do everything with you in mind
You haunt me *

You Know

You know
you could make me beg
harder than he can

you see it in my eyes
in the way I move
and laugh
and touch him

if only I'd look your way
if only I'd notice you looking at me
if only I'd look into your eyes
I'd know it too *

I Just Realized

I just realized
you have a crush
on me
I just saw past
your hi-how-are-you smile
your friendly hug *

Think of Me

Think of me while I think of you
imagine touching me
 while I imagine touching you
you'll know when I'm playing
body first, then brain
play too, or pass

it's harmless
it's fun
it's safe
it's sexy
there are no rules
no physical contact
no money exchanged
no repercussions
no regrets
no misunderstandings
no awkwardness *

Sue Schafer

You Must Be Busy

You must be busy today
too busy to play
I sought you out this morning
from the warmth of my bed
I stretched my mind
released my imagination
I couldn't feel you
couldn't sense you
there were no breaks
in your concentration
no space for me
I didn't persist
I moved on
now I'm a bit anxious
a bit concerned
I have never felt so completely
cut off
you had to have done it intentionally
you are doing it now
you have never done this to me before
no one has *

I've Got a Crush

What Happened

What happened?
Why have you totally shut me out?
I know you want me on your own terms.
When it 's convenient - when you are not busy.
But you're always busy – it's never convenient.
You'll just have to adjust.
You'll just have to perform daily functions while com-
pletely captivated by your thoughts –
your imagination –
by a dream –
by an unattainable fantasy that becomes more tangible
- more compelling –
more undeniable every day.
I know you like thinking about me.
I know you like feeling my body with your mind.
I know you like how your body feels when you think
about mine.
I know you haven't abandoned me - you can't aban-
don me.
You've gone too far.
The sensations are too mesmerizing
The wanting too strong.*

Sue Schafer

I Felt My Future Open

I felt my future open
before I saw it
It was
as if
a cliff
suddenly appeared
and then
the next thing
I knew
I let you
press
your
lips
against
mine *

Your Body is Beautiful

Your body is beautiful, you could be in the movies, he says over and over again. He rubs his hands up and down the back of my legs and up along my spine. He taps the wooden rice paddle against my butt - hard enough to get my attention. I want more of your time.

/I'll see what I can do. My day calendar is always full.

/How about sometime after 4pm? We could have happy hour. A little private time and then see what happens. Perhaps dinner, a movie, time with other people. What do you do during the day?

/I'm busy.

/Doing what?

/This and that.

/Like what?

/Like why do you want to know?

/I'm curious. I want to know all about you.

(Oh, Oh. Here we go. First a little knowledge, then a little participation, then a little input, then a little control. I hope I'm being too cynical.)

/I want to integrate myself into your everyday life. I don't want control over you or your schedule. I just want to be with you. To go with you to the grocery store, to the mall, to the movies. I want to have coffee with you during the day, a cocktail at a swanky bar, I want to exercise with you. I want to be your best friend. I want us to be inseparable.

/I enjoy being with you too. You have to understand that my spending time with other people or doing things without you doesn't mean I don't want to be with you.

/What else could it mean?

/Sorry, my girlfriend just called. I've got to go. *

It Was So Much Fun

It was so much fun
flirting
smiling
fantasizing

Why is there suddenly so much
awkwardness
anguish
self consciousness

I feel like I've lead you on
like I've hurt your feelings
but how could this be

maybe I'm feeling guilty
maybe I'm feeling vulnerable
maybe I need to break it off

but how can I

we've never spoken

Sue Schafer

Shocked

Why was I so shocked to see that woman
openly smile and lock eyes with you
Why did I believe that I was the only one who has
crushes
fantasies
longings
desires

I felt jealousy
rage
anger
fear
insecurity
hatred

You didn't notice me in your bubble
Your bubble of bliss

You were too lost in a world of urgent love, lust, sex,
romance

I'm not relevant in your fantasy world
like you're not relevant in mine *

About the Author

Sue Schafer and her husband Charlie live in Helena, Montana, and Kuala Lumpur, Malaysia. Sue is originally from Honolulu, Hawaii.

Contact Sue Schafer at:

suesueschafer@hotmail.com

POB 582
Helena MT 59624 USA

One Residency A-1-3
No. 1 Jalan Nagasari
50200 Kuala Lumpur MY

www.ingramcontent.com/pod-product-compliance
Lightning Source LLC
Chambersburg PA
CBHW030012040426
42337CB00012BA/752